M000012535

AS CLOSE

AS A SISTER

Thoughts and

Scripture

to Celebrate

our Friendship

inspirio™

I don't think you realize what an incredible blessing you are in my life (although you've never been one to brag). With countless kind words and simple gestures you've brought joy to many of my grayest hours. So, today, this very moment, I want to make sure you know that you mean the world to me. Life just wouldn't be the same without you as my friend.

Friendship is the breathing rose,
with sweets in every fold.

OLIVER WENDELL HOLMES

ૐ

*Perfume and incense bring
joy to the heart,
and the pleasantness
of one's friend
springs from his earnest counsel.*

PROVERBS 27:9

ૐ

*A faithful friend is a strong defense;
And she that has found her
has found a treasure.*

LOUISA MAY ALCOTT

When the song of my heart goes silent,
  you sing it again and remind me
When the light in my eyes grows dark,
  you lift up my head to the sun
And when the joy all around seems
  to escape me, you capture it in your arms
And with a hug, you share it with me.

MOLLY DETWEILER

Grace, mercy and peace from
Jesus Christ, the Father's Son,
will be with us
in truth and love.

2 JOHN 3

One sister have I in our house,
And one a hedge away,
There's only one recorded
But both belong to me.

One came the way that I came
And wore my past year's gown,
The other as a bird her nest,
Builded our hearts among.

She did not sing as we did,
It was a different tune,
Herself to her a music
As Bumble-bee of June.

To-day is far from childhood
But up and down the hills
I held her hand the tighter,
Which shortened all the miles.

EMILY DICKINSON

A blessed thing it is to have a friend;
one human soul whom we can trust utterly;
who knows the best and the worst of us,
and who loves us, in spite of our faults:
who will speak the honest truth to us,
while the world flatters us to our faces,
and laughs at us behind our backs;
who will give us counsel and will comfort
and encourage us in the day of difficulty.

CHARLES KINGSLEY

O n the road between
the homes of friends,
grass does not grow.

NORWEGIAN PROVERB

How rare and wonderful is that flash
of a moment when we realize we have
discovered a friend.

WILLIAM ROTSLER

୨ବ

F*rom your corner of the world*
You reached out with your loving words
And with your gentle manner
And you touched my heart.

ANONYMOUS

୨ବ

E*very good and perfect gift is*
from above, coming down
from the Father
of the heavenly lights.

JAMES 1:17

We are as close as sisters because...

We don't feel like we have to do our hair or put on makeup before we get together.

If I laugh too hard and accidentally snort, it's okay (it just makes us both laugh harder).

If I cry and my nose gets runny, you simply offer me a tissue and keep hugging me.

We can talk about anything, everything, and nothing and never bore, offend, or irritate each other.

You give me hugs for no reason at all that take me by surprise and warm my heart!

&

In all my prayers for ... you, I always pray with joy.

PHILIPPIANS 1:4

*F*aithful no matter what comes

*R*elaxing, together, as chums

*I*nspiration to face each
new day

*E*ncouragement for when
skies are gray

*N*ice to talk with
all the day long

*D*evoted to a friendship
that's strong.

Blessed is the influence of one true,
loving soul on another.

GEORGE ELIOT

ஜ

A good deed is never lost;
She who sows courtesy reaps friendship,
And she who plants kindness gathers love.

ST. BASIL

ஜ

Give, and it will be given to you.
A good measure, pressed down,
shaken together and running over,
will be poured into your lap.
For with the
measure you use, it
will be measured to you.

LUKE 6:38

I always feel that the great high privilege, relief and comfort of friendship is that one has to explain nothing.

KATHERINE MANSFIELD

❦

You always know what I'm feeling
By the tone of my voice
By the look on my face
By some soft whisper in your heart

You always know what I'm needing
The words that will encourage
The smile that will brighten
And the soft whisper that will
heal my heart.

MOLLY DETWEILER

A friend into whose heart we may pour out our souls, and tell our corruptions as well as our comforts, is a great privilege.

GEORGE WHITEFIELD

Two are better than one,
because they have a good return
for their work:
If one falls down,
his friend can help him up.
But pity the man who falls
and has no one to help him up!

ECCLESIASTES 4:9–10

In meeting again after a separation, acquaintances ask after our outward life, friends after our inner life.

MARIE VON EBNER-ESCHENBACH

The Gifts of a Best Friend

A lifetime of love in a hug and a smile;

A reason to visit and stay for a while.

The strength of a bond that's destined to last,

The joys of the present and the warmth of the past.

These are the treasures a fortunate few

Are lucky to cherish all their lives through.

These are the blessings on which we depend,

For these are the gifts of a very best friend.

The best kind of friend is the one you could sit with, hardly saying a word, and then walk away feeling like that was the best time you've ever had. It's a special joy to have someone you can be quiet with.

MOLLY DETWEILER

ૐ

A true friend understands
even what you don't say.

ૐ

A friend loves at all times.

PROVERBS 17:17

A companion loves some agreeable qualities which a person may possess, but a friend loves the person.

JAMES BOSWELL

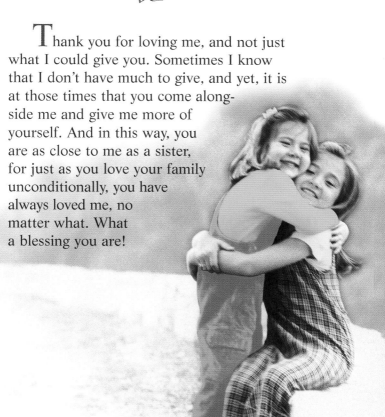

Thank you for loving me, and not just what I could give you. Sometimes I know that I don't have much to give, and yet, it is at those times that you come alongside me and give me more of yourself. And in this way, you are as close to me as a sister, for just as you love your family unconditionally, you have always loved me, no matter what. What a blessing you are!

Your Friendship is a Blessing

Your friendship is a blessing—
It's your very best you share,
Your talents and your wisdom,
And your capacity to care.
You're always there to lend support,
Whatever needs arise,
You're always making sure that others know
That they're special in your eyes.

Your friendship is a blessing,
And, to all who are your friend,
It's one of the most precious gifts
That life could ever send!

AUTHOR UNKNOWN

I value a friend who for me finds room on his calendar, but I cherish the friend who for me does not consult his calendar.

ROBERT BRAULT

❧

*You seem to always
have time for me, even in
the midst of your full and busy life.
I can't begin to express
how grateful I am for the gift
of your time to me in all
those moments that I
needed you the most.*

❧

When a friend asks,
there is no tomorrow.

GEORGE HERBERT

I ask these
blessings for you,
my dearest friend ...

May the LORD repay you for what you have done. May you be richly rewarded by the LORD.

RUTH 2:12

May you be blessed by the LORD,
the Maker of heaven and earth.

PSALM 115:15

❧

May God be gracious
to us and bless us
and make his face shine upon us.

PSALM 67:1

❧

May God himself,
the God of peace,
sanctify you through and through.
May your whole spirit, soul and body
be kept blameless at the coming
of our Lord Jesus Christ.

1 THESSALONIANS 5:23

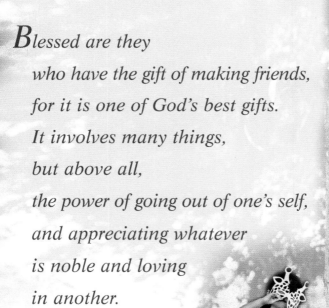

Blessed are they
who have the gift of making friends,
for it is one of God's best gifts.
It involves many things,
but above all,
the power of going out of one's self,
and appreciating whatever
is noble and loving
in another.

THOMAS HUGHES

My friends have made the story of my life. In a thousand ways they have turned my limitations into beautiful privileges, and enabled me to walk serene and happy in the shadow.

HELEN KELLER

G*reater love
has no one than this,
that he lay down his life
for his friends.*

JOHN 15:13

If I could reach up and hold a star
for every time you've made me smile,
the entire evening sky would be in the
palm of my hand.

AUTHOR UNKNOWN

ℰᴈ

Those who are wise
will shine like the brightness of the heavens,
and those who lead many to righteousness,
like the stars for ever and ever.

DANIEL 12:3

ℰᴈ

*Those who bring sunshine
into the lives of others
cannot keep it from themselves.*

J.M. BARRIE

*M*ay the sun always shine
on your windowpane,
May a rainbow be certain
to follow each rain.
May the hand of a friend
always be near you,
May God fill your heart
with gladness to cheer you.

<small>IRISH BLESSING</small>

You know me like no one else does. You've seen me when I was on top of the world and you danced and laughed with me. You've been there when I was near despair and you let me cry in your arms. You have cheered me on to achieve great things and gently helped me get back on the right track when I was wrong. In so many ways I would be a lesser person without your friendship. What a wonderful gift you are in my life!

❧

The heart
benevolent and kind
the most
resembles God.

ROBERT BURNS

*In friendship,
every burden is light.*

JOHN GAY

❦

Friendship doubles your joys
and divides your sorrows.

AUTHOR UNKNOWN

❦

We are so very rich if we
know just a few people
in a way in which we
know no others.

CATHERINE BRAMWELL-BOOTH

We must ever be friends; and of all who offer you friendship let me ever be the first, the truest, the nearest and dearest.

HENRY WADSWORTH LONGFELLOW

In the triangle of love between ourselves, God and other people, is found the secret of existence, and the best foretaste, I suspect, that we can have on earth of what heaven will be like.

SAMUEL M. SHOEMAKER

෴

Though one may be overpowered,
two can defend themselves.
A cord of three strands is not quickly broken.

ECCLESIASTES 4:12

෴

Christian friendship is
a triple-braided cord.

ANONYMOUS

Lord,
  Keep my friend in your arms
  As I keep her in my prayers.
  Send sunshine her way today
  And lift her up.
  Amen.

༄

May the God of hope fill you with all joy and peace as you trust in him, so that you may overflow with hope by the power of the Holy Spirit.

ROMANS 15:13

༄

A little word of kindness spoken,
  A motion or a tear,
  Has often healed the heart that's broken,
  And made a friend sincere.

DANIEL CLEMENT COLESWORTHY

I love you, my friend.
Not only for what you are.
But for what I am
When I am with you.

I love you,
Not only for what
You have made of yourself,
But for what
You are making of me.

I love you
For the part of me
That you bring out.

ROY CROFT

Whenever you're having one of "those" days when nothing seems to go right, and no matter how hard you try, you can't seem to make those around you happy, remember what a blessing you are to me. You are my encourager when I'm discouraged, and my comforter when I'm most uncomfortable. You can always bring laughter through my tears and show me my strength in the midst of my weakness. *Remember that* whenever you need encouragement, comfort, laughter and strength.

*M*ercy,
peace and love
be yours
in abundance.

JUDE 2

*To the world
you might be one person,
but to one person
you might be the world.*

AUTHOR UNKNOWN

୫ର

*A kind heart is a fountain of gladness,
making everything in its vicinity
freshen into smiles.*

WASHINGTON IRVING

୫ର

Kind words are the music of the world. They have a power which seems to be beyond natural causes, as if they were some angel's song which had lost its way and come to earth.

FREDERICK WILLIAM FABER

I'd like to be the sort of friend
   that you have been to me

I'd like to be the help
   that you've always been glad to be;

I'd like to mean as much to you
   each minute of the day

As you have meant, old friend of mine,
   to me along the way.

EDGAR A. GUEST

Some people come into our lives
and quickly go. But some stay
and leave their smile, their kind words,
and their love upon our hearts.
And we are never, ever the same.

AUTHOR UNKNOWN

There are incredible, life-changing moments,
when you find a special friend—someone
who changes everything for the better, just
by being there. She makes you believe
that there is really good in the world after all.
I discovered that kind of friend
the day I met you.

My prayers for you...

I pray that you, being rooted and established in love, may have power, together with all the saints, to grasp how wide and long and high and deep is the love of Christ, and to know this love that surpasses knowledge— that you may be filled to the measure of all the fullness of God.

EPHESIANS 3:17–19

The LORD bless you
and keep you;
the LORD make his
face shine upon you
and be gracious to you;
the LORD turn his
face toward you
and give you peace.

NUMBERS 6:24–26

*U*pon your heart like paper white,
Let none but friends presume to write;
And may each line with friendship given
Direct the sender's thoughts to Heaven.

AUTHOR UNKNOWN

Insomuch as
any one pushes you
nearer to God,
she is your friend.

ANONYMOUS

Blessings A to Z

My dear friend,
these are the blessings I wish for you:

Abundant life

Beauty in each new day

Creativity in the face of challenges

Dreams that come true

Encouragement when times are tough

Faithful friends by your side

God's grace to fill your soul

Health in body, mind, and spirit

Inspiration to soar to new heights

Joy unspeakable

Kisses and hugs

Love that overwhelms you

Miracles both big and small

New discoveries and adventures

Opportunities to spread your wings

Peace that passes understanding

Quiet times to rest and pray

Rewarding work and play

Strength when you feel like giving up

Time to read or garden or chat

Unity in all your relationships

Vision for what could be

Wisdom when facing big decisions

X-tra dessert on a tough day

Yesterday's failures forgotten

Zest for life always!

MOLLY DETWEILER

When the curtains of night are pinned back by stars,
And the beautiful moon leaps in the skies,
And the dewdrops of heaven are kissing the rose,
It is then that my memory flies
As if on the wings of some beautiful dove
In haste with the message it bears
To bring you a kiss of affection and say:
I'll remember you, friend, in my prayers.

AUTHOR UNKNOWN

I always thank my God
as I remember you
in my prayers.

PHILEMON 4

Friendship is precious, not only in the shade, but in the sunshine of life; and thanks to a benevolent arrangement of things, the greater part of life is sunshine.

THOMAS JEFFERSON

૪ઃ

Never shall I forget the time which I spent with you. Continue to be my friend as you shall always find me yours.

AUTHOR UNKNOWN

૪ઃ

The Lord be with us as we walk
Along our homeward road;
In silent thought or friendly talk
Our hearts be near to God.

JOHN ELLERTON

The sun
The stars
And the moon above
Are not as wonderful
As a friend's kind love.

୫ର

A friend is someone who
can make you laugh when you
think you'll never smile again.

୫ର

Precious things,
in this world, are very few.
That is the reason
there is just one you.

෯෧

From the fullness
    of God's grace we have
    all received one blessing
    after another.

JOHN 1:16

෯෧

Scatter your seeds of kindness
    All enriching as you go—
Leave them. Trust the Harvest Giver;
    He will make each seed grow.
    So until the happy end
Your life shall never lack a friend.

AUTHOR UNKNOWN

*The best mirror
is an old friend.*

GEORGE HERBERT

⁊ↄ

Thank you for helping me to see myself truly, even when the truth wasn't always pretty. You've always helped me see my true worth and beauty while gently showing me where I needed improvement. Perhaps I haven't always seemed grateful, but deep down, I always am.

⁊ↄ

*God has made
everything beautiful in its time.*

ECCLESIASTES 3:11

Some of us know what it is to love,
and we know that could we only have our
way, our beloved ones would be over-
whelmed with blessings. All that is good,
and sweet, and lovely in life would be
poured out upon them from our lavish
hands, had we but the power to
carry out our will for them.
And if this is the way of love
with us, how much more
must it be so with our God,
who is love itself.

HANNAH WHITALL SMITH

We have shared
> Laughter and fears
> Pizza and tears
> Coffee and chats
> Our present and past

We have endured
> Boring teachers and bad perms
> Breakups and mid-terms
> Lost loves and failed dreams
> Empty wallets and pimple creams

Through it all we
> Giggled and screamed
> Sighed and dreamed
> Fought and forgave
> And tried to behave

And because of this you'll always be
> The one who can always make me grin
> Who I'll count on through thick and thin
> My friend with whom I'll never part
> The precious sister of my heart.

MOLLY DETWEILER

May you and I
always be *as close as sisters,*
bound together by shared
joys and sorrows,
memories of laughter and tears,
and *a deep love*—for
each other and for
our Father in heaven.

At Inspirio
we love to hear from you—
your stories, your feedback, and your product ideas.

Please send your comments to us by way of e-mail at icares@zondervan.com or to the address below:

Attn: Inspirio Cares
5300 Patterson Avenue SE
Grand Rapids, MI 49530

inspirio

If you would like further information about Inspirio and the products we create please visit us at:

www.inspiriogifts.com

Thank you and God Bless!